You and Me

by Lynne Rickards
illustrated by Connah Brecon
and Andrew Painter

Morning

"Wake up, wake up!" the sunbirds say,
"It's time to start another day!"
I yawn and stretch and scratch my head,
Then pull my brother out of bed.

"Wake up, wake up! The day's begun.
Get up so we can have some fun!"
My brother blinks and rubs his eyes,
And hears the sunbirds' morning cries.

We dress and eat and find our shoes,
Then run outside – no time to lose!
The morning chores must all be done
Before the heat of midday sun.

All finished – now we're free to play!
We find some shade to spend the day.
He catches frogs, I dip for fish,
We make believe and make a wish.

My wish is this – I'll make no other:
May I always have my brother.

My Sari

By Debjani Chatterjee

Saris hang on the washing line:
A rainbow in our neighbourhood.
This little orange one is mine,
It has a mango leaf design.
I wear it as a Rani would.
It wraps around me like sunshine,
It ripples silky down my spine,
And I stand tall and feel so good.

You and Me

Eyes of brown
Eyes of blue
You see me and I see you.

Hair of jet
Hair of gold
Both of us are six years old.

Bit by bit
Day by day
More and more we laugh and play.

Up and down
To and fro
Playground races – off we go!

Now we're quiet
Take a look –
Snuggled down to read a book.

Arm in arm
Side by side
Our two smiles are big and wide!

Best of friends
You and me
That is what we'll always be.

Suki

When Suki was a kitten,
She was just a ball of fluff.
She tried to climb the curtains
But she wasn't big enough.

She climbed half-way and then got stuck,
And Mama had to save her.
She didn't fare much better
With a ball of string we gave her.

When Suki was a kitten,
She was curious and brave.
Each cardboard box and narrow space
Was like a secret cave.

She'd crawl inside and sniff about
In search of hidden treasure.
To find a bug or bottle cap
Would give her so much pleasure!

Now Suki is a grown-up cat –
She's long and sleek and clever.
Her fur is like a tiger
And her eyes can stare forever.

She's just as brave and curious
But now she takes her time.
She looks before she leaps
When there's a fence she wants to climb.

Our Suki loves to curl up close
And let me stroke her fur.
There's nothing I like better –
And just listen to her purr!

Our Lollipop Man

Our Lollipop man is called Donald MacDonald.
His hair is as white as the snow.
He's quite a bright fellow,
All decked out in yellow –
We cross when he says we can go, you know,
We cross when he says we can go.

Our Lollipop man plays his bagpipes at weddings
(Or birthdays, if business is slow).
He really looks smart in
His pink-and-green tartan
And puts on a fabulous show, you know,
He puts on a fabulous show.

Our Lollipop man is a colourful character –
Wouldn't you say it was so?
And if we're in trouble
He's there on the double –
A wonderful person to know, you know,
A wonderful person to know.

Mr. Bing

Mr. Bing is fantastic.
He can cut the world in two.
He can make a live volcano.
He can catch a kangaroo!

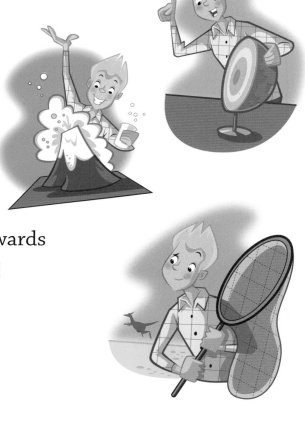

Mr. Bing is clever.
He can multiply by eights.
He can count by sevens backwards
And do sums on roller skates!

Mr. Bing is funny.
He can always make us smile.
We love his tie collection –
He has such a crazy style!

We think school is brilliant
And it's down to just one thing.
The greatest teacher ever –
Our amazing Mr. Bing!

Oath of Friendship

Anon, China

Shang ya!
I want to be your friend,
For ever and ever without break or decay.
When the hills are all flat
And the rivers are all dry,
When it lightens and snows in summer,
When Heaven and Earth mingle –
Not till then will I part from you.

Home Time

The final bell is ringing
And we're packing up our books.
We crowd into the cloakroom
Pulling jackets off their hooks.

We spill into the playground
Like a stampede – here we come!
I search the grown-up faces.
I am looking for my Mum.

I see some other parents
Where they always stand and wait.
But *my* Mum – where is *my* Mum?
She is never, ever late.

At last I see her running!
I am running too, and then –
She picks me up and hugs me.
Everything is right again.

15

Ode to My Oldest Best Shoes

By Kwame Dawes

Soft and just the right shape too,
My feet slip in, my toes are giggling,
They know how to make a ball swerve
They get green with grass
And brown with mud
And black with soot
And wet with rain
And smelly and grey
And still feel as right as can be.

There is no sweating or straining
No moaning and groaning
To get my feet to slip right in
It's as if I am floating
Or dancing a jig
Barefoot in cotton
Through nettles and thorns
Through garbage heaps

Over nails and grass
And still feel as right as can be.

That's why I am crying like a baby
And limping like a jalopy truck*
That is why my toes are whining
That they can't breathe or laugh at all
No dirt, no dust
No stones in the toes
No paint and grease
No games in the bush
I'll never feel right again, Mum,
Not with these awful new shoes, Mum,
Not with these awful new shoes!

* Jalopy truck old truck in bad condition.

Evening Feast

The nicest time of every day
Is when we come together.
We've all been hard at work and play
In cold and wintry weather.

We gather onions for the pot
And peas and carrots too.
The salty water's getting hot –
tonight we're making stew.

Our Mama fries a bit of meat.
She lets potatoes simmer.
Before too long it's time to eat
Our very tasty dinner!

Outside, the chilly winter storm
Is blowing from the east.
We gather close, all safe and warm
And share our evening feast.

Three Little Boats

Three little boats,
One, two, three,
Sailing on a sudsy sea.

Three little boats,
Red, yellow, blue.
A storm is brewing – what to do?

Here come the waves,
Big and tall,
Swooping down to splash them all.

Here comes a shark,
Circling near ...
Hurry, let's get out of here!

Little red boat,
In a spin –
A giant whirlpool sucks it in!

Little yellow boat,
Lost at sea,
Washes up on my island knee.

Little blue boat,
Tossed and blown,
Drifts behind me all alone.

Come, little boats,
The sea is rough!
Bathtub storms are always tough!

Come, little boats,
You're safe from harm.
Shelter in my harbour arms.

Imagine

Last night I went to Timbuktu and wrestled with a bear.
The night before I battled with a dragon in his lair.
I sometimes sail a pirate ship across the Seven Seas.
Or fly a magic carpet high above the tangled trees.

Some nights I'm in a jungle with an elephant beside me.
Sometimes I go to outer space with only stars to
 guide me.
I jump on trains and aeroplanes and follow where
 they lead.
A good imagination and my Dad are all I need.

Blue

Now it's time to dim the lights,
Snuggle down and say goodnight.
I've put my books and toys away,
All ready for another day.
I've washed and dried and brushed and spat,
I've kissed my mum and stroked the cat.
There's only one thing left to do –
To fall asleep, I must have Blue.

Blue is soft and fits just right
Curled up beside me every night.
He never snores, he's good as gold,
And though he's worn and getting old,
I love him more than all the rest.
Of all my toys, old Blue is best.
I close my eyes and hold him tight,
And whisper in his ear, "Goodnight ..."

You and Me ● Lynne Rickards

Teaching notes written by Sue Bodman and Glen Franklin

Using this book

Content/theme/subject

'You and Me' is a poetry anthology focused on family and friendship. The poems in this book reflect a range of experiences across ages and cultures, providing opportunity to compare and contrast ways in which the themes are explored.

Language structure

- A range of poetic styles are used, appropriate to subject and setting.
- Sentence structures are varied in order to convey feelings, and to support reading aloud with rhythm and prosody.

Book structure/visual features

- Different structural features are used, such as varying line length, rhyming patterns and layout on the page.
- Illustrations support the main theme of each individual poem within the anthology.

Vocabulary and comprehension

- Opportunity to explore rhyme and syllabification, and consider effect in oral reading.
- Use of imagery and poetic, figurative language to convey meaning.

Curriculum links

PSHE – Use this book in studies about how people live: families, friendship, people who help us.

Literacy – Children can explore other poetry anthologies, considering different ways in which these are compiled (for example, poems for specific age groups, or around certain topics). Children could compile their own anthologies, with favourite poems to make up the collection.

Learning outcomes

Children can:

- identify different patterns of rhyme and verse in poetry
- explore poetry writing conventions, considering the effect across the different poems
- compare and contrast poems on similar themes, considering preferences and giving rationales.

Planning for guided reading

Lesson One: Poetry styles and conventions

Give a copy to each child in the group. Read the title and blurb together. Discuss how this book varies from others they have read in guided reading lessons: it is not a story or a non-fiction book. What do they notice about this particular book's layout?

Discuss the notion of a poetry anthology as a collection of works complied by the poet him/herself or by an editor. You may have other poetry anthologies to show the children.

There is no contents list, so ask the children to flick quickly through the book, looking at the titles of the poems. Then ask: *Why do you think the anthology is called 'You and Me'?* Point out poems related to family (e.g. *'Morning'*, p.2; *'Evening Feast'*, p.18), friendship (*'Oath of Friendship'*, p.13) and caring (*'Suki'*, p.8; *'Our Lollipop Man'*, p.10).

Turn to the poem entitled *'Morning'* on pp.2-3. Explore the poem's structure of four-line verses with rhyming couplets on lines one and two, and lines three and four. Note also how the final verse only has two lines, and the effect this creates for the reader. Point out how each first line starts with a capital letter, even though it may be a